Two large lions, having fun.
Through the grass they run and run.

3

In the forest, **three** bears **scurry**.
Why are they in such a **hurry**?

Four elephants stomp in a row,
Marching high and marching low.

Five crocodiles go swimming past.
These snappy friends are very fast.

5

Six pandas have no time for lunch.
They'd rather run than
munch and crunch!

Seven foxes leap around,
They jump and dart along the ground.

Eight little penguins hop and glide,
In the sea they splash and slide.

8

Nine swooping parrots fly up high,
And speed their way across the sky.

Ten monkeys swing their tails with ease
As they go leaping through the trees.

The animals all think it's funny...
They're being chased by one small BUNNY!

"TAG! You're it!"